I0465100

BLESSINGS
AN INSPIRATIONAL
COLORING BOOK

R.R. Russell

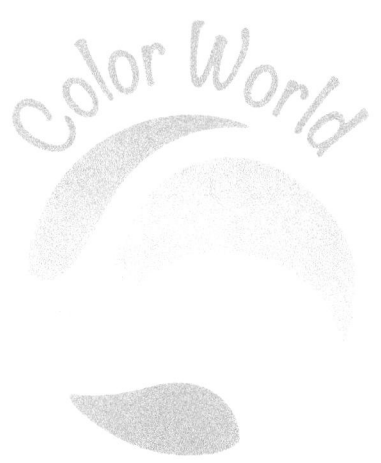

Morning Gate Press
P.O. Box 652
Spanaway, WA 98387

ISBN-13:
978-1522937487

ISBN-10:
152293748X

To:_____

_____

From:_____

_____

Date:_____

_____

Color World

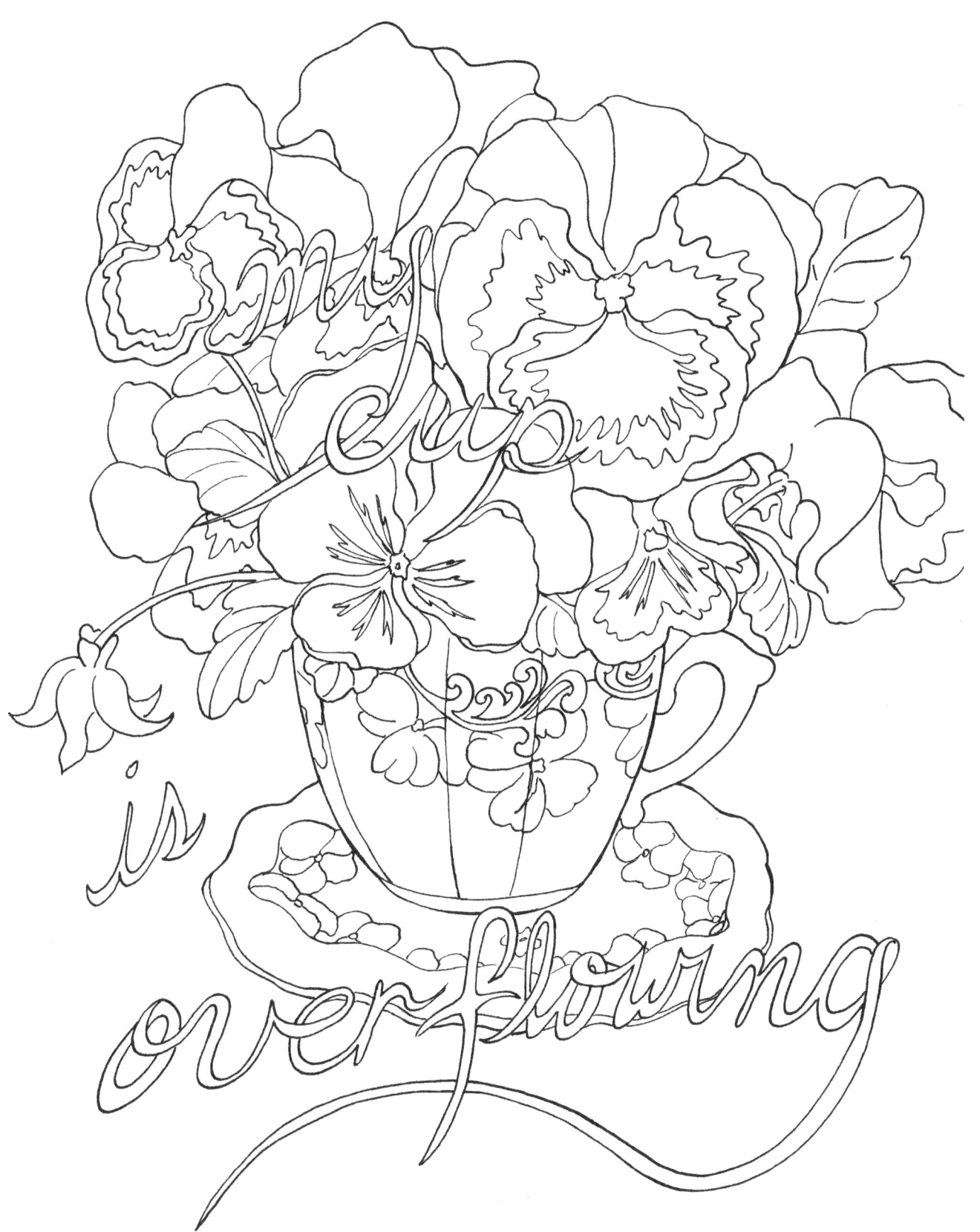

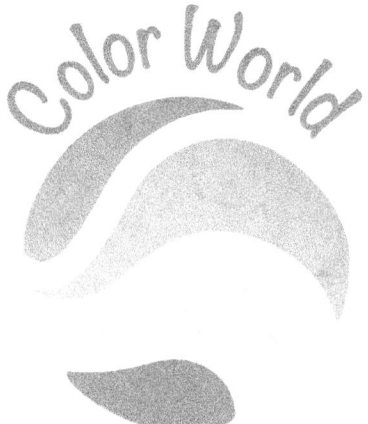

All other ground

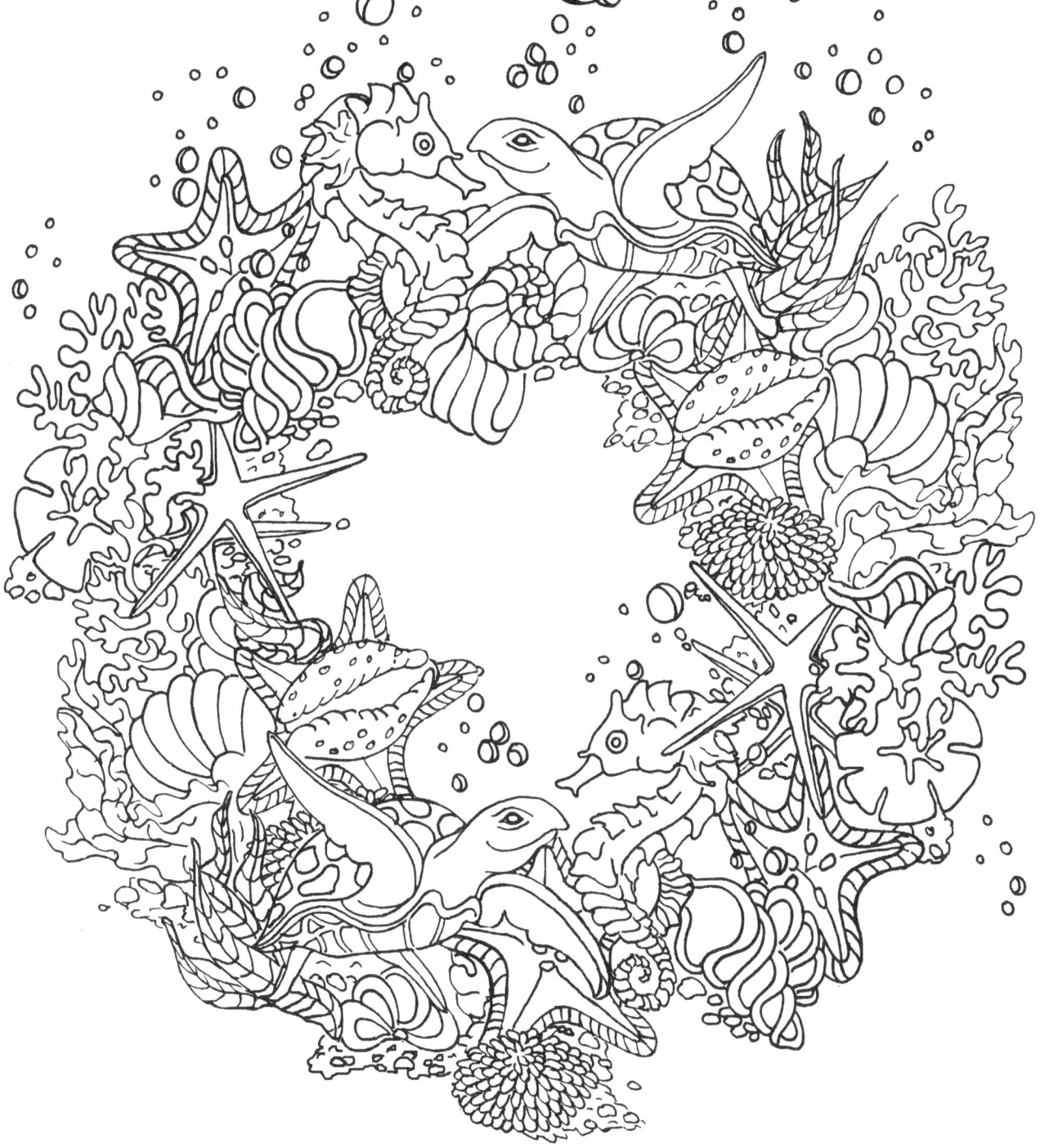

is sinking sand

Color World

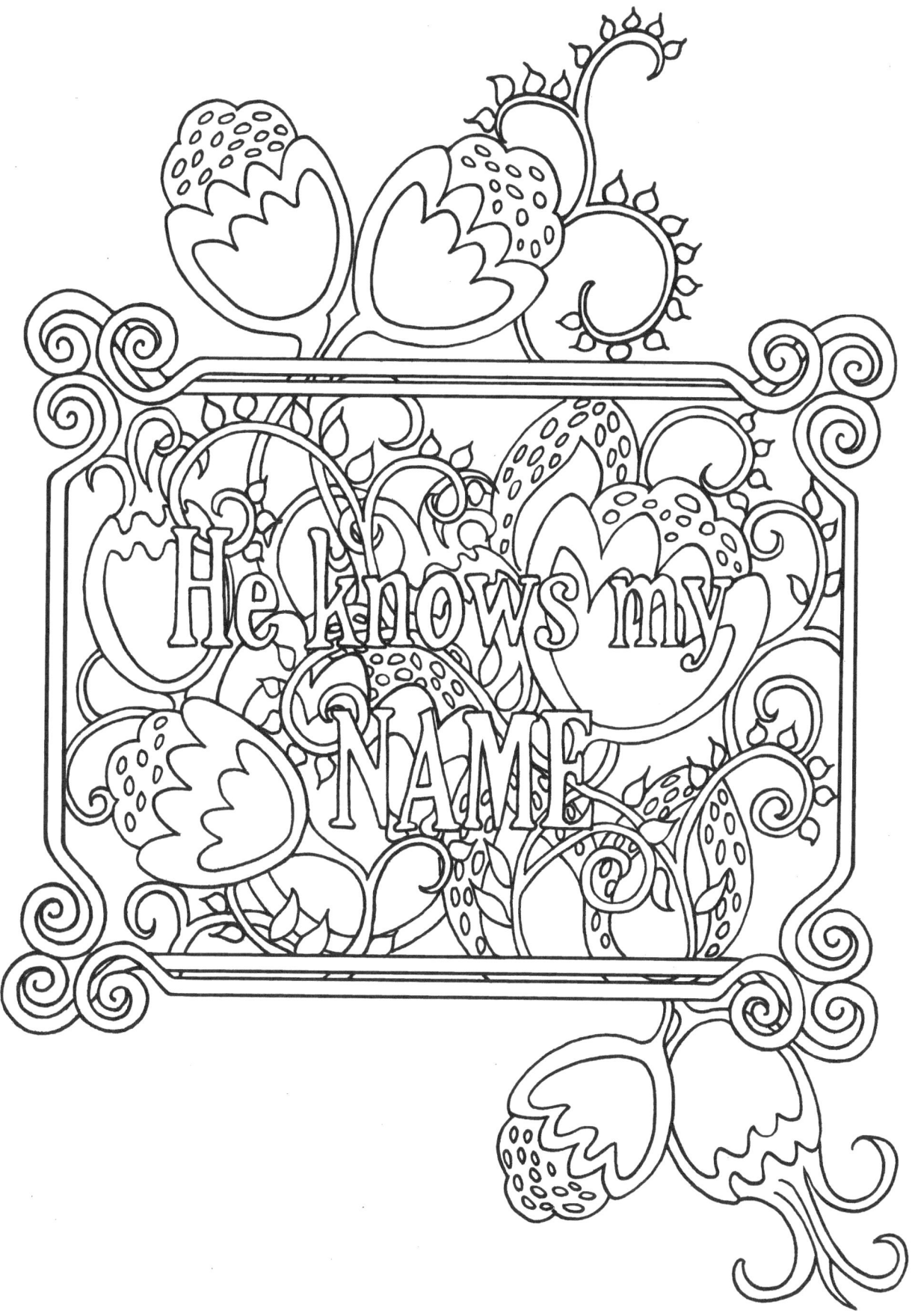

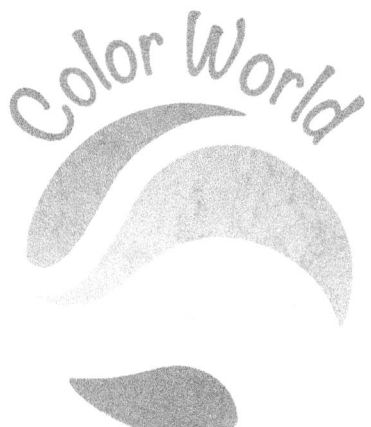

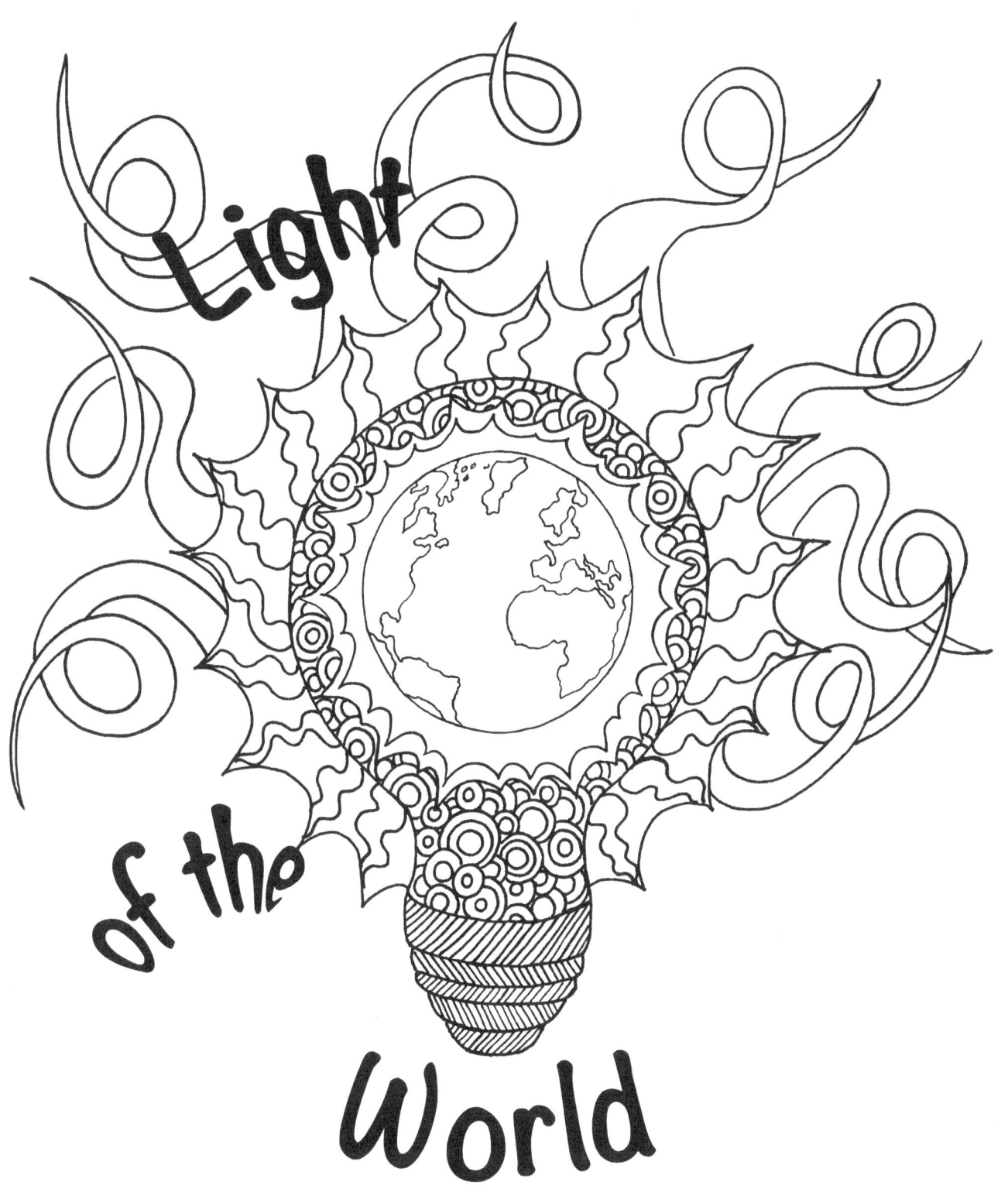

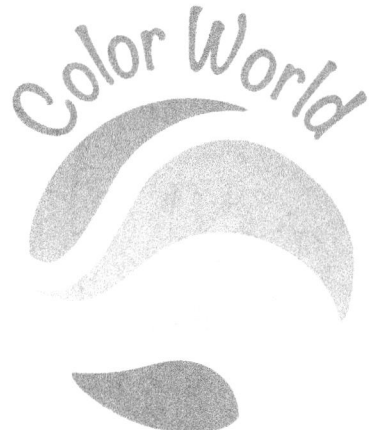

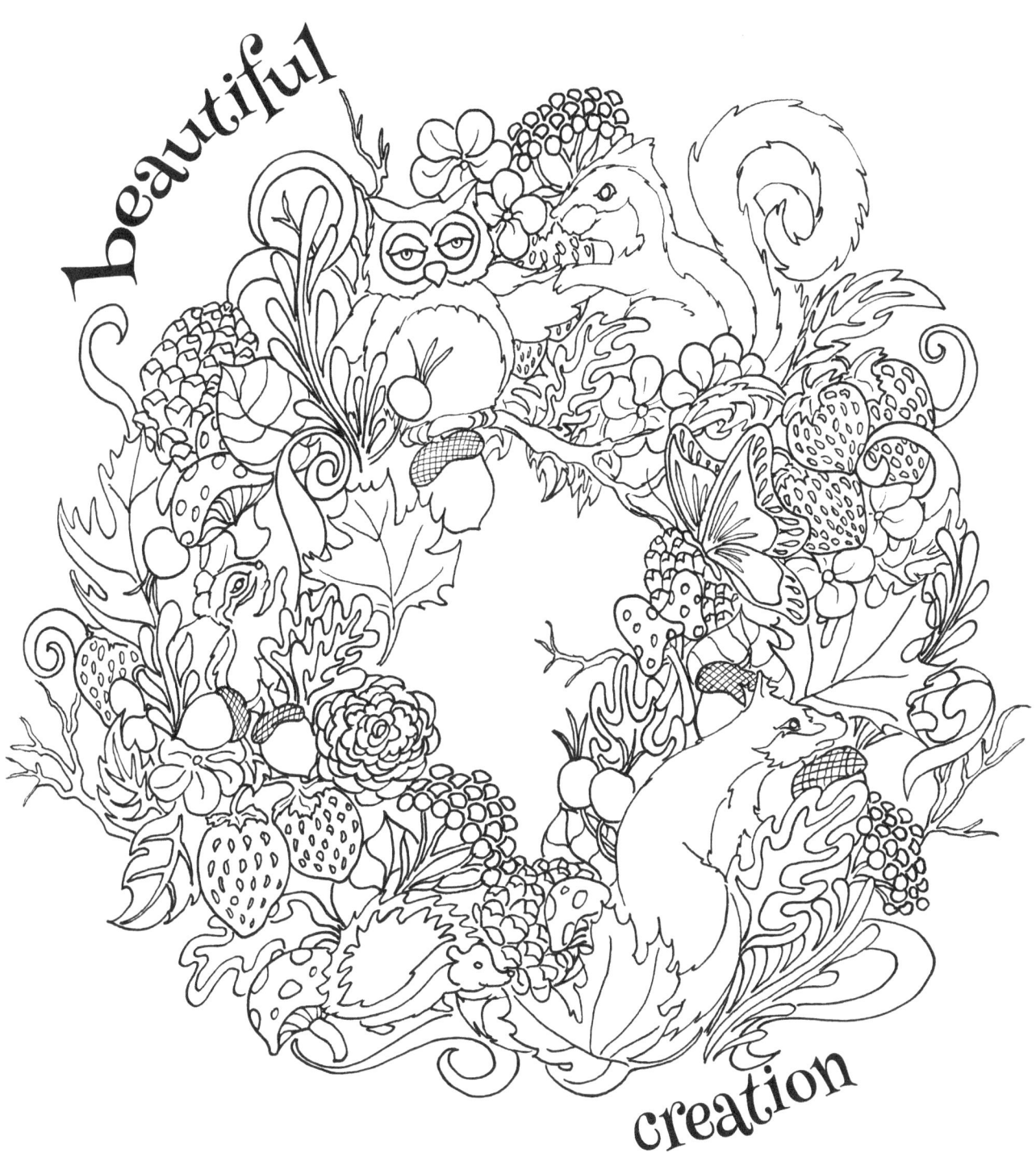

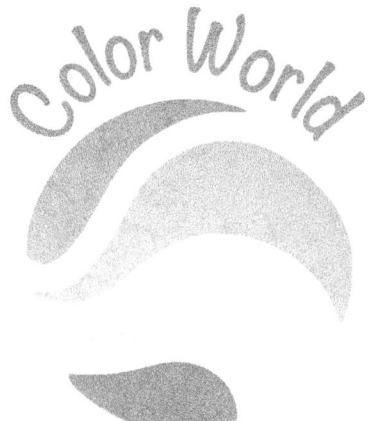

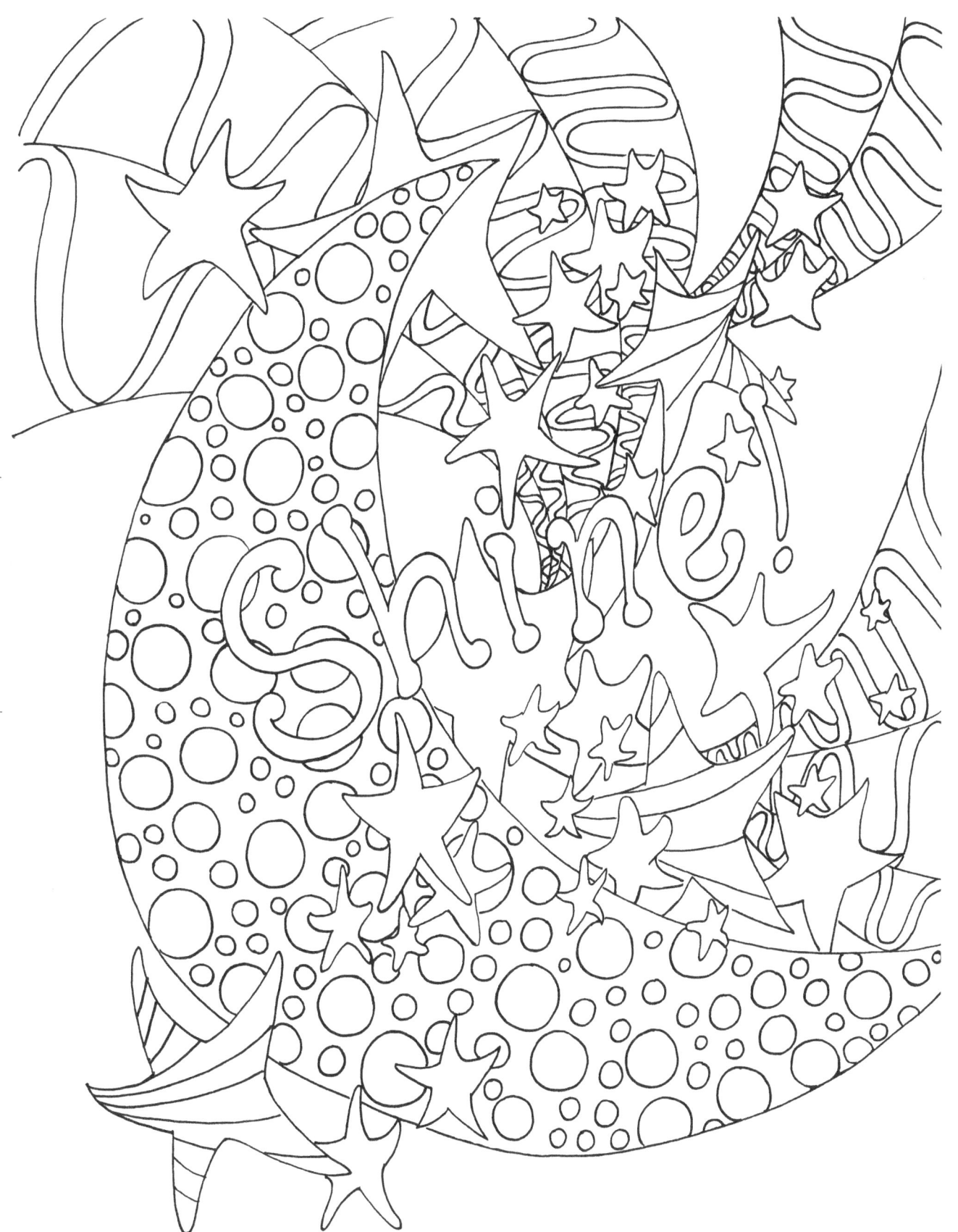

Color World

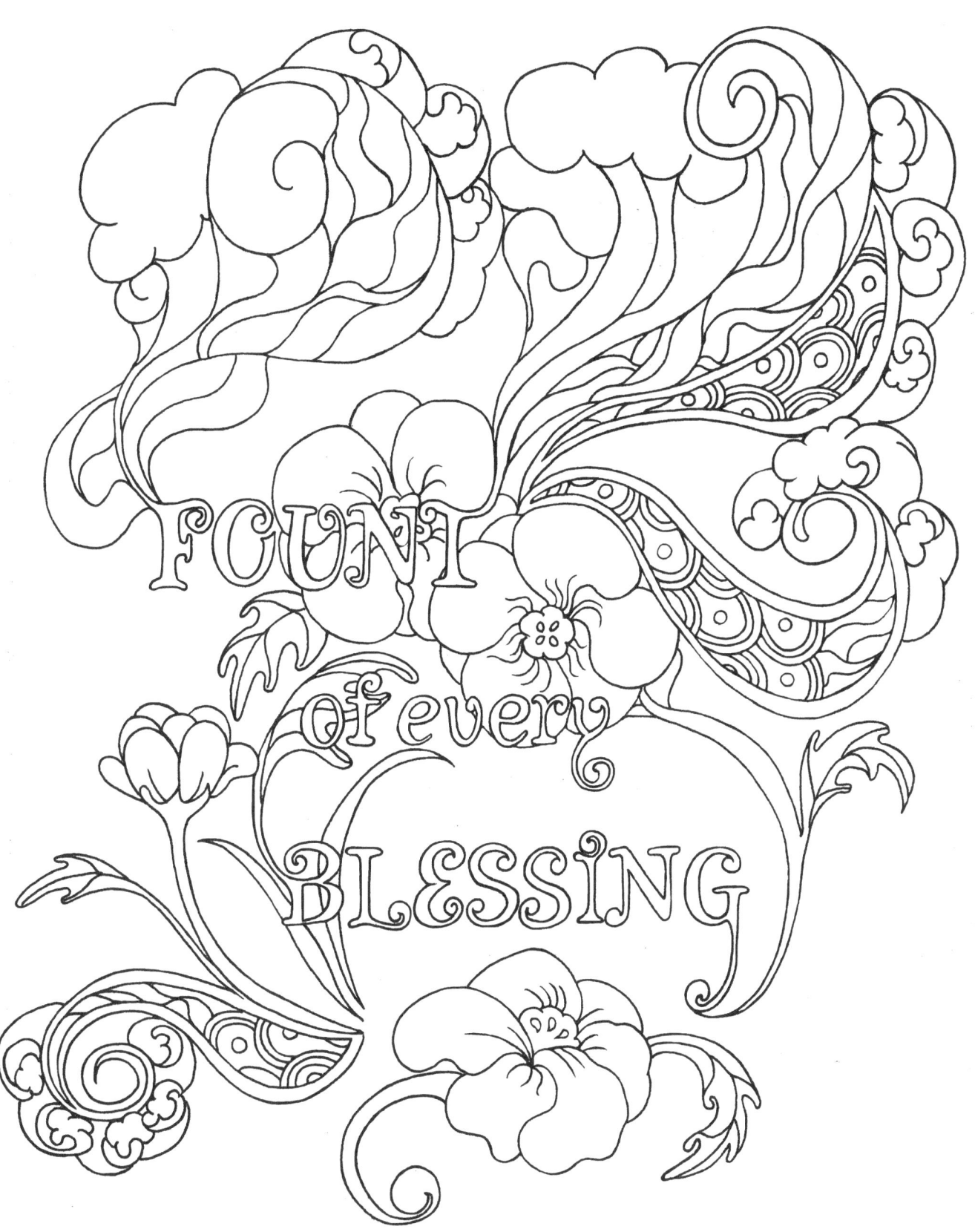

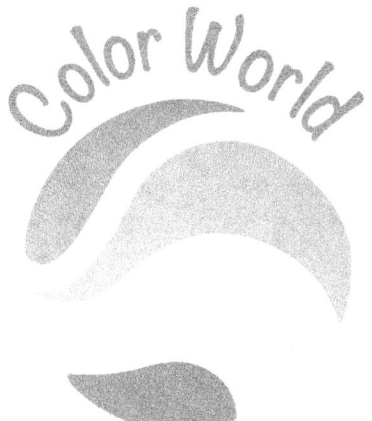

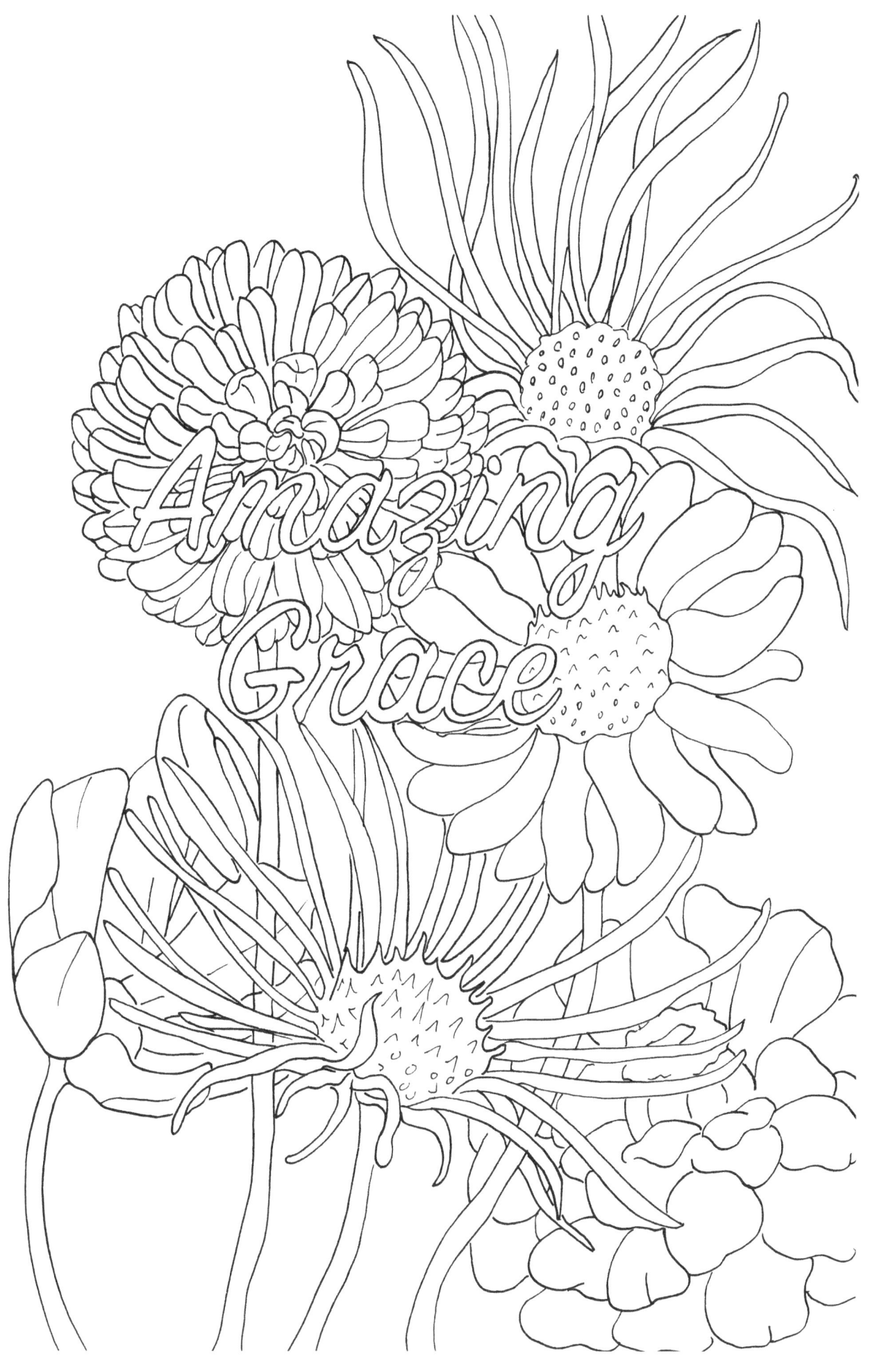

Color World

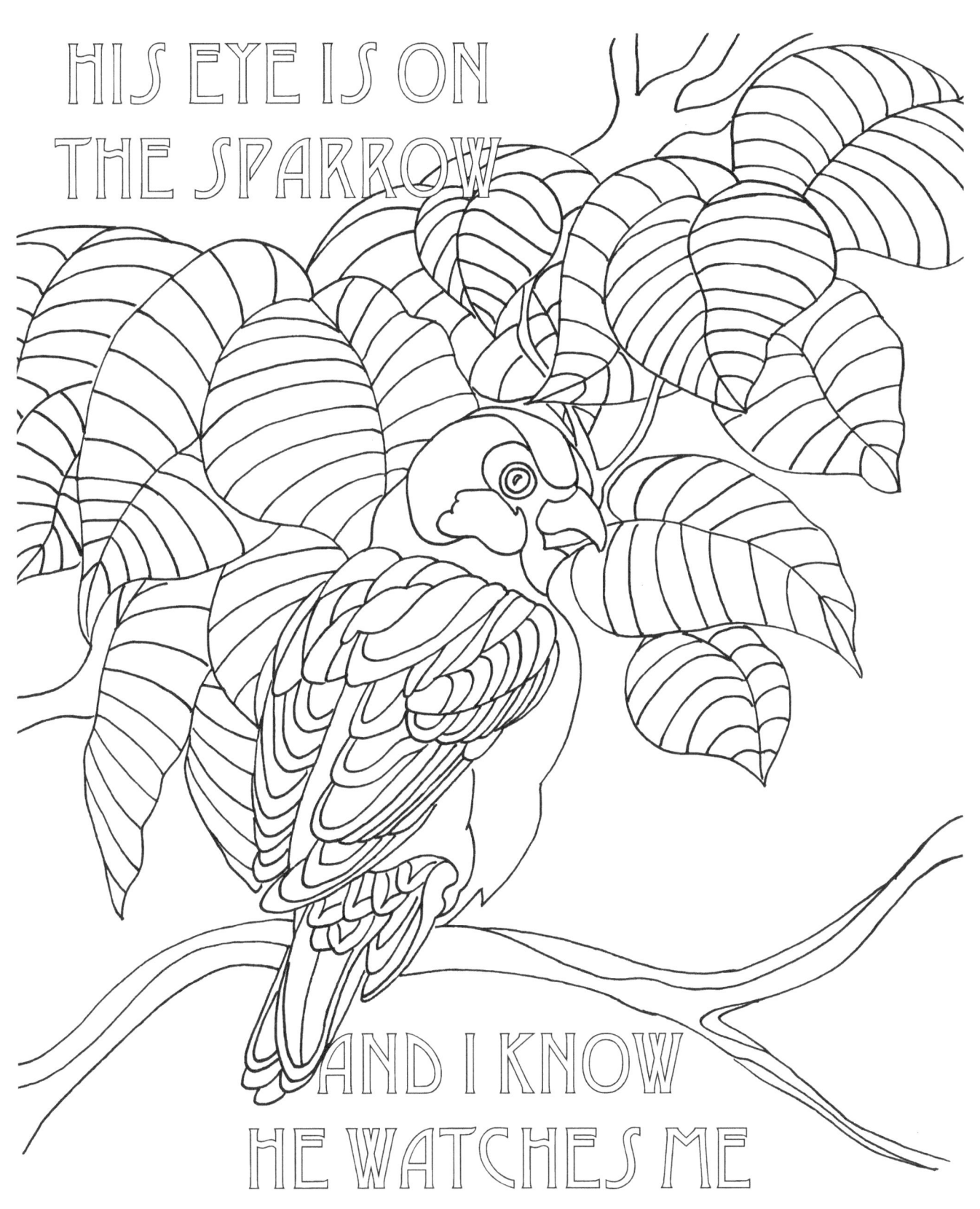

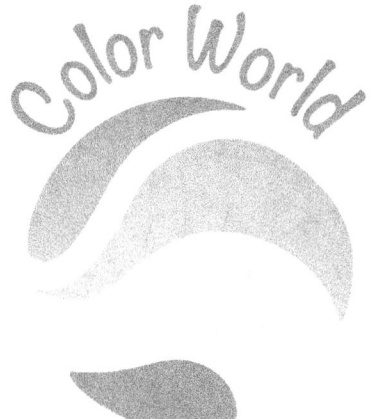

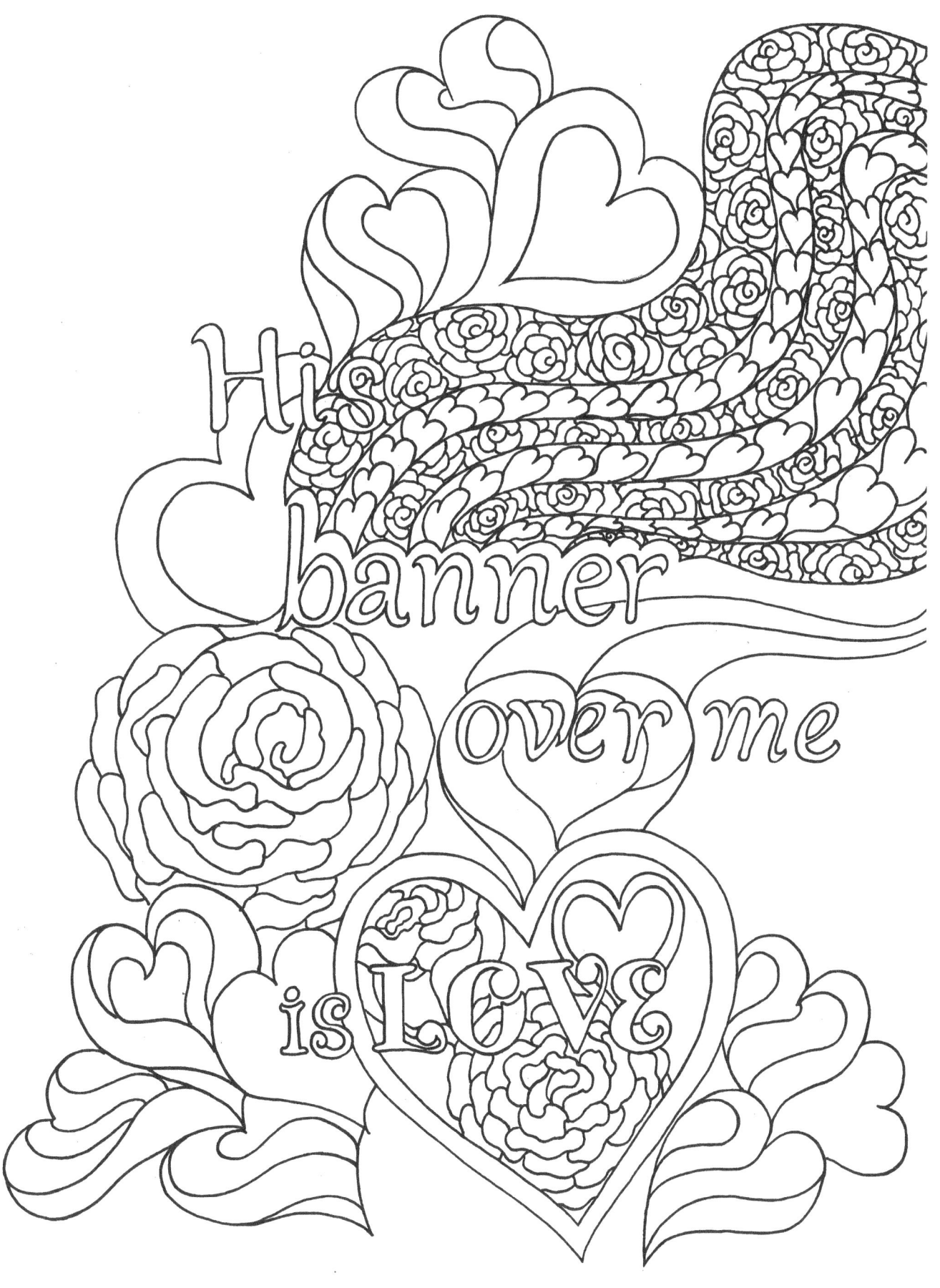

Color World

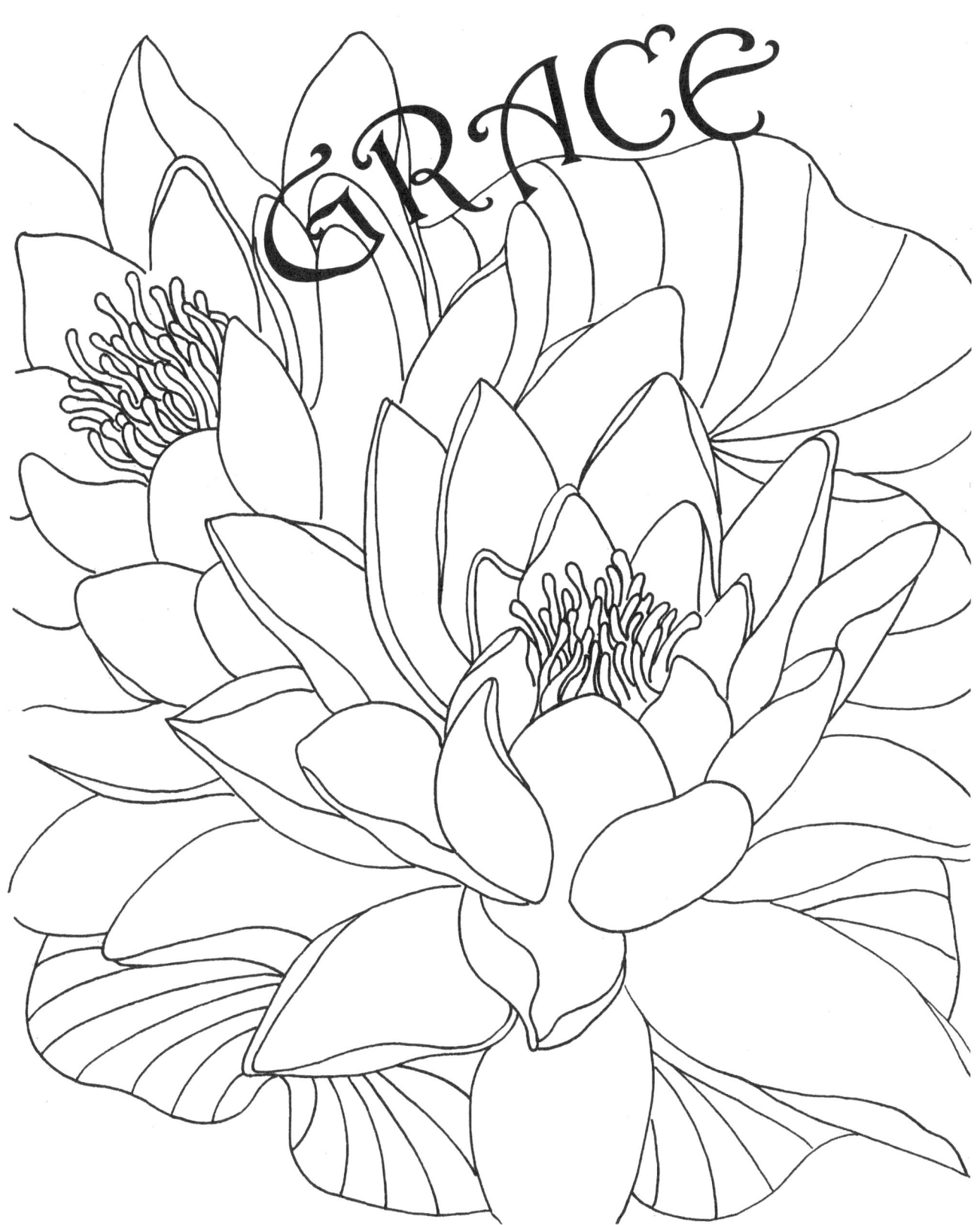

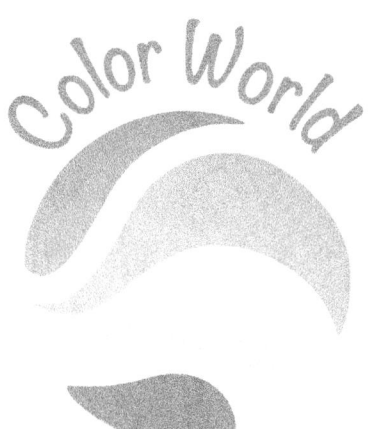

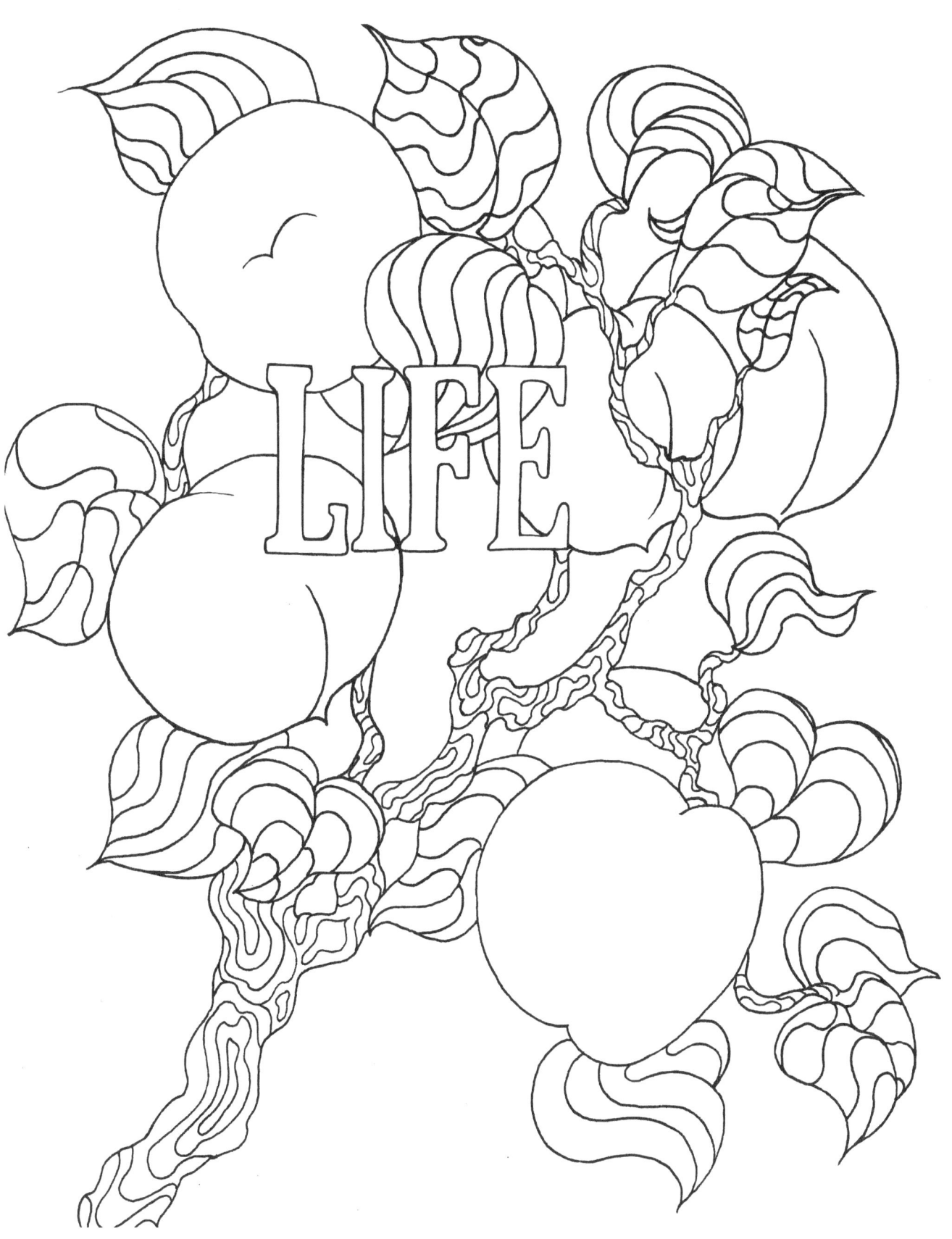

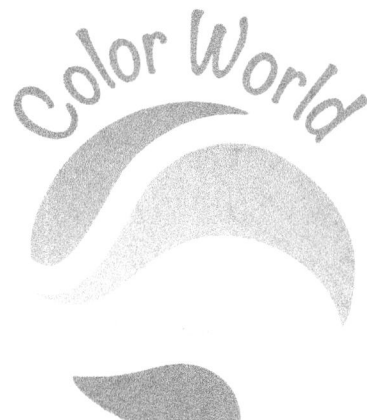

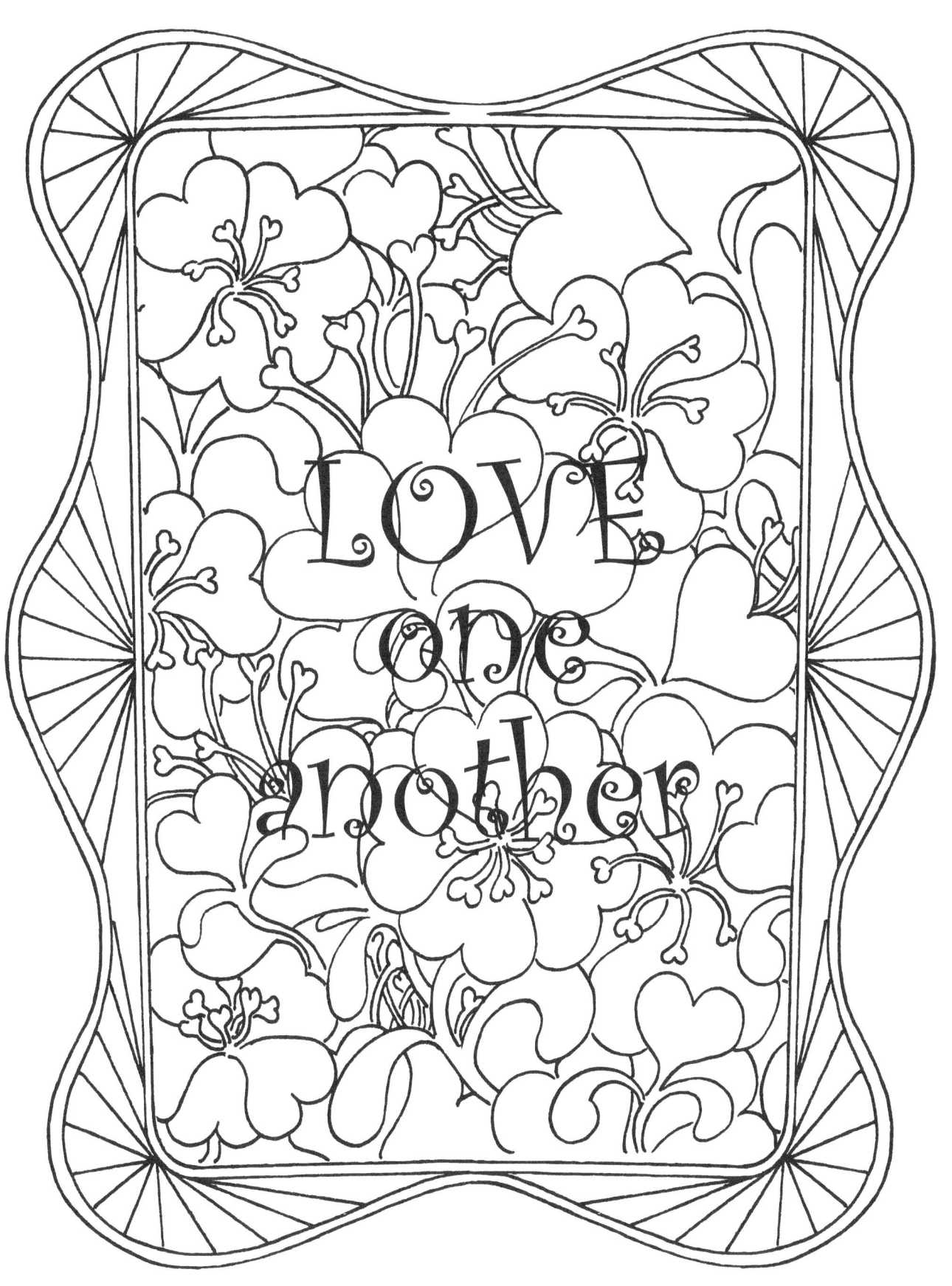

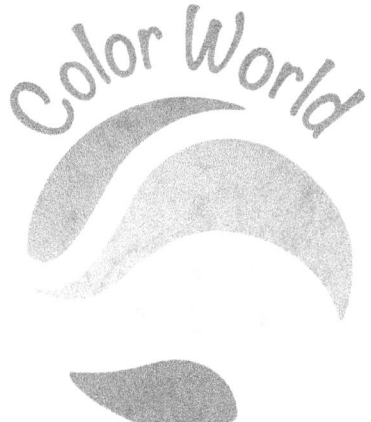

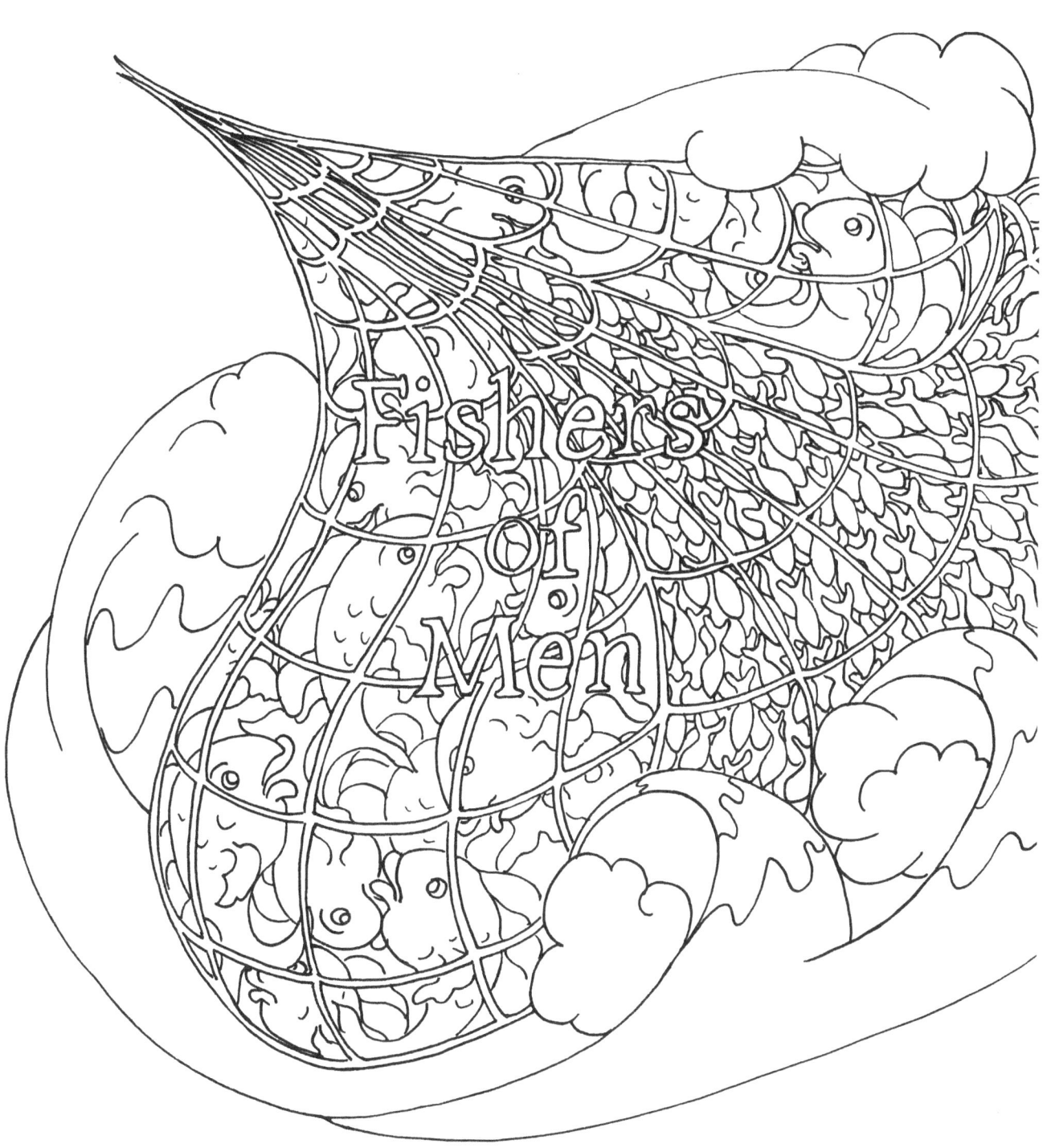

Color World

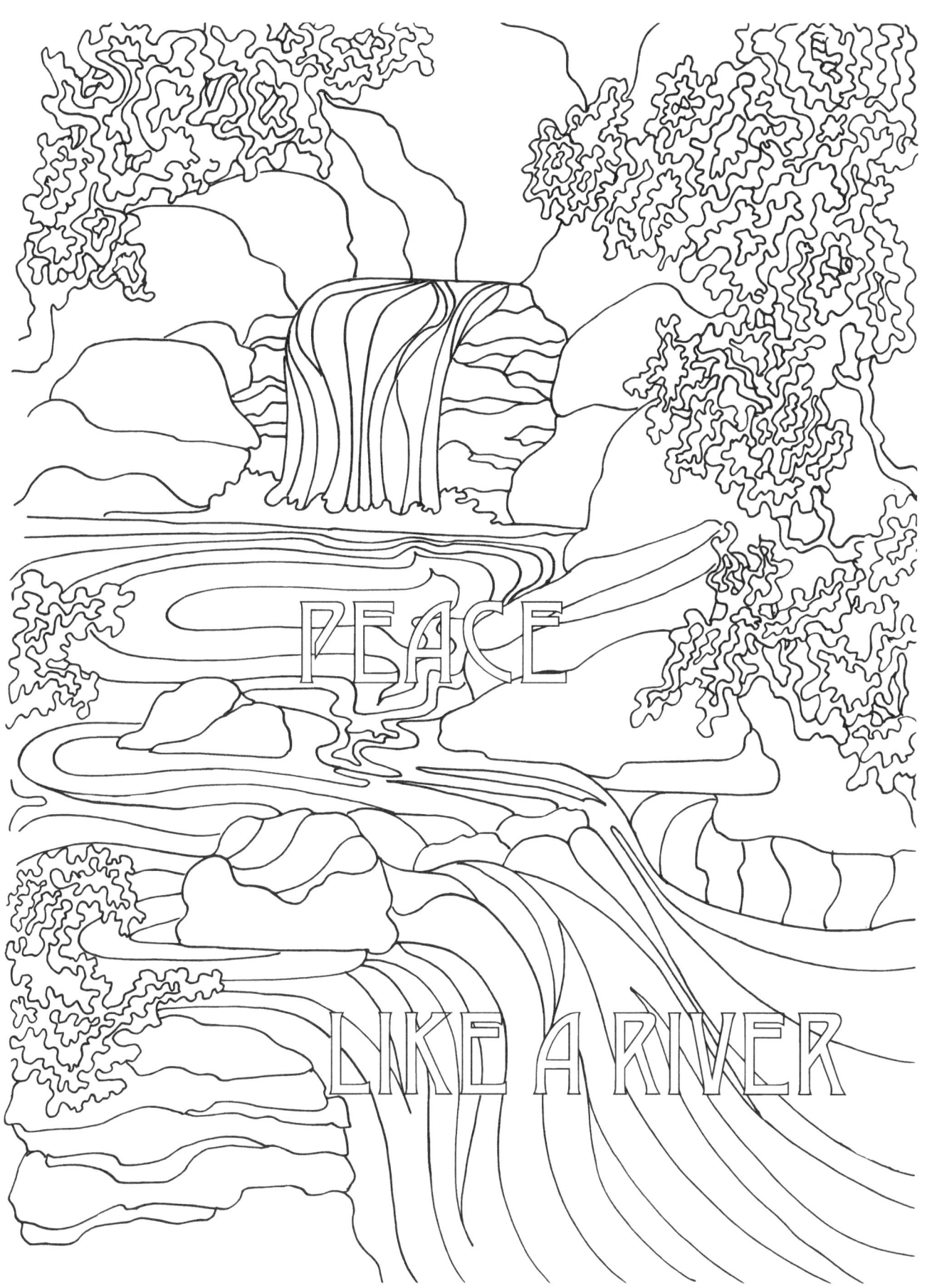

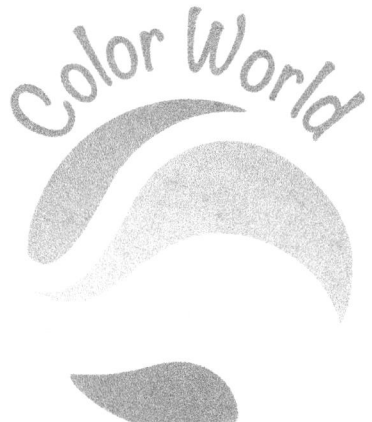

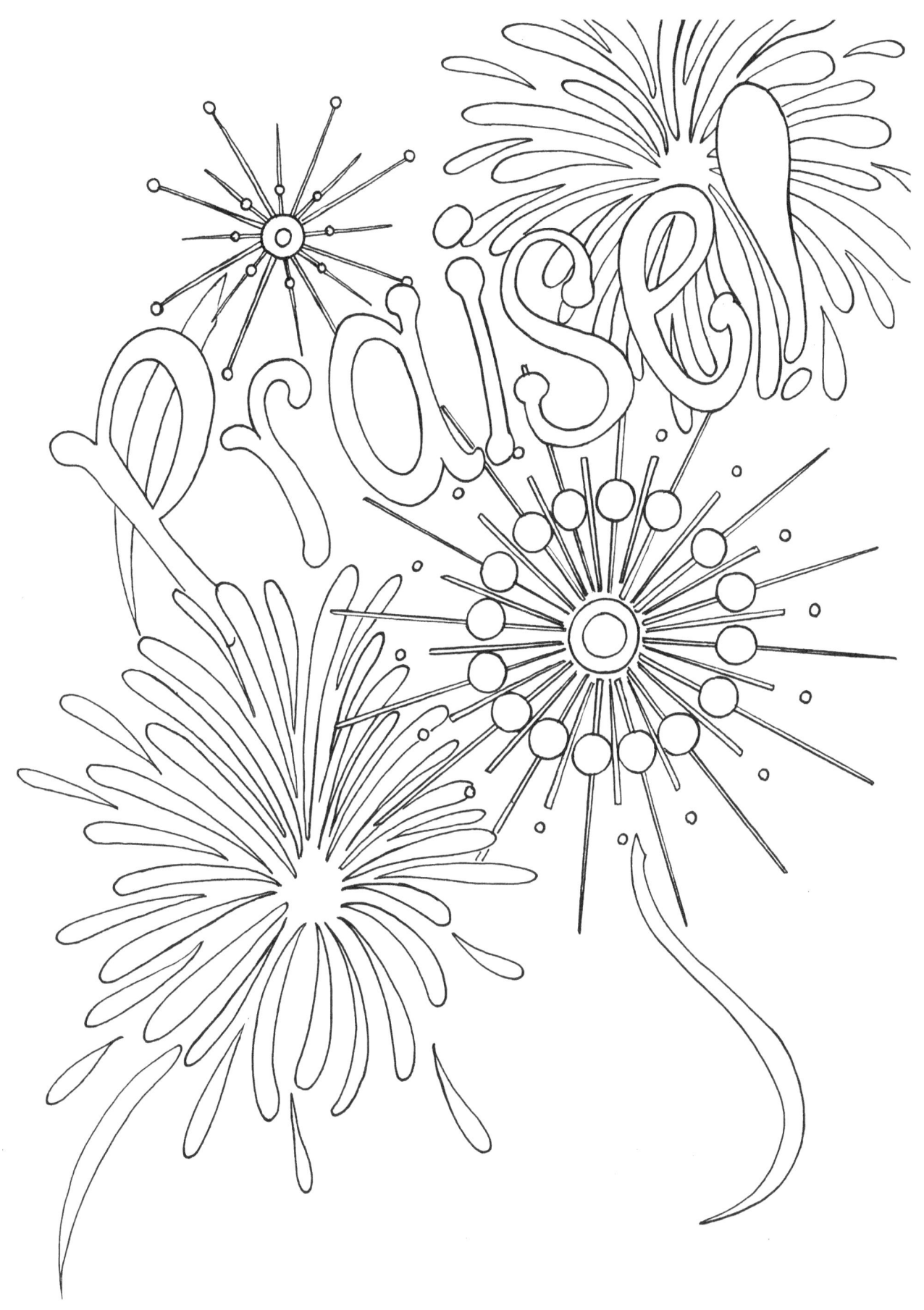

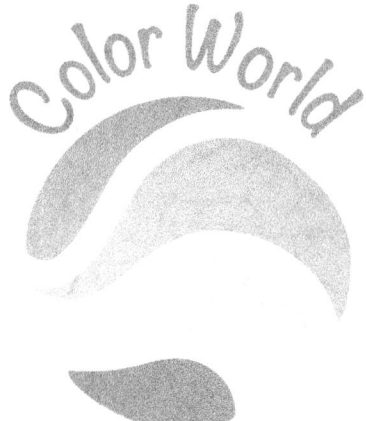

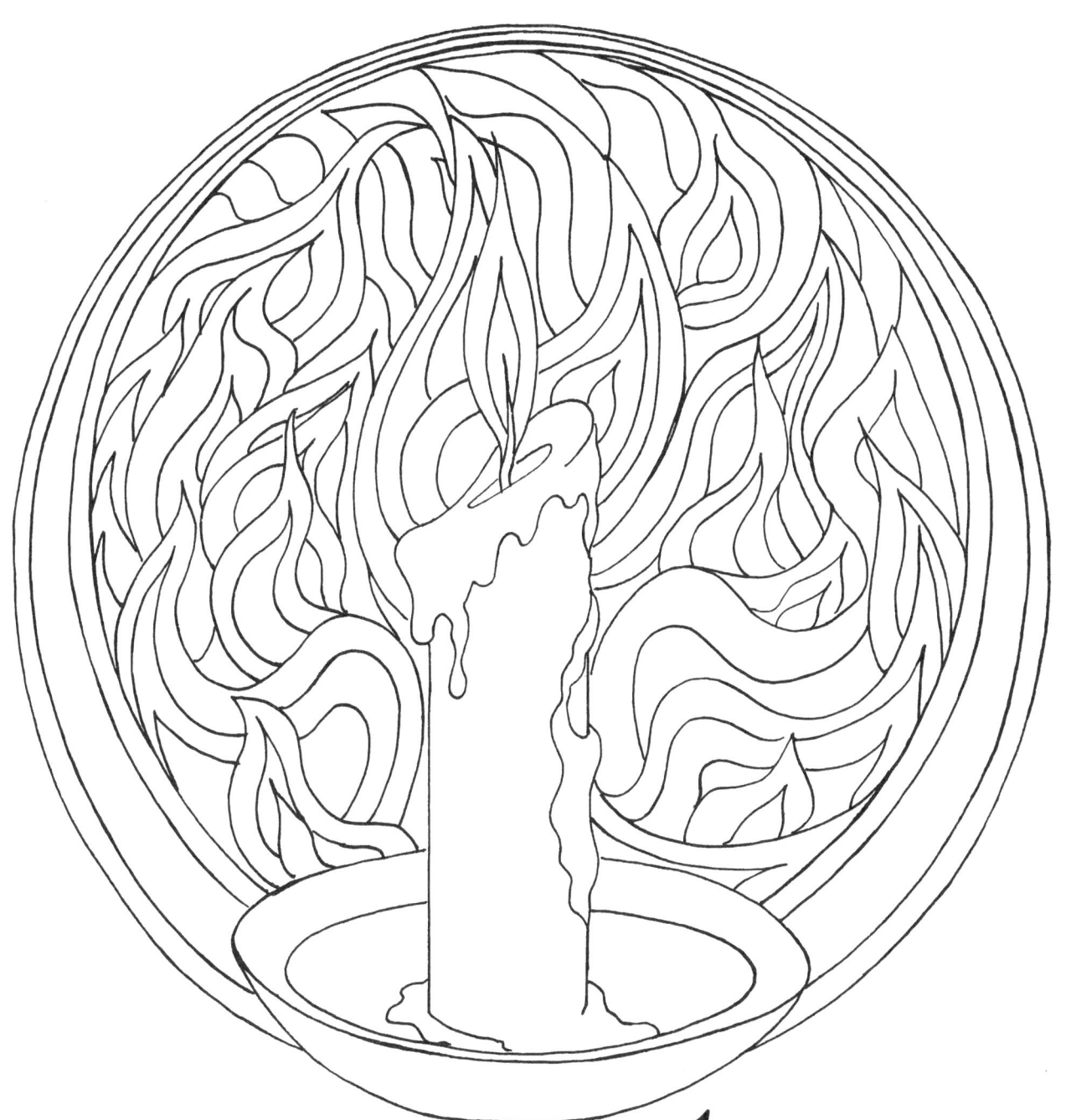

Be a light

Color World

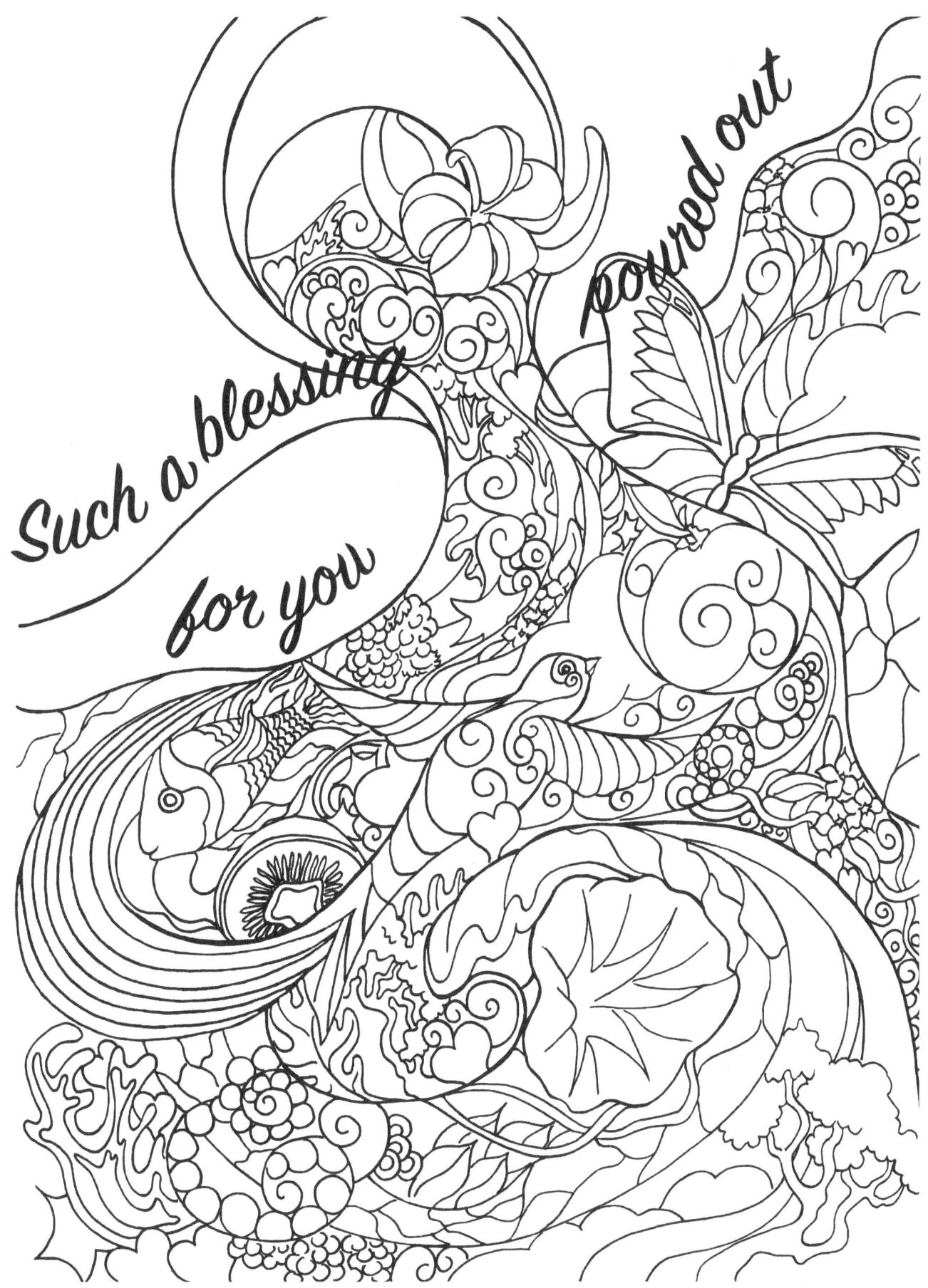

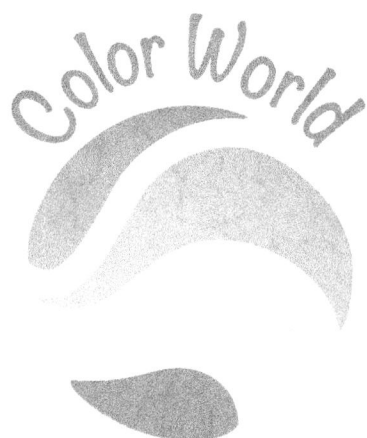

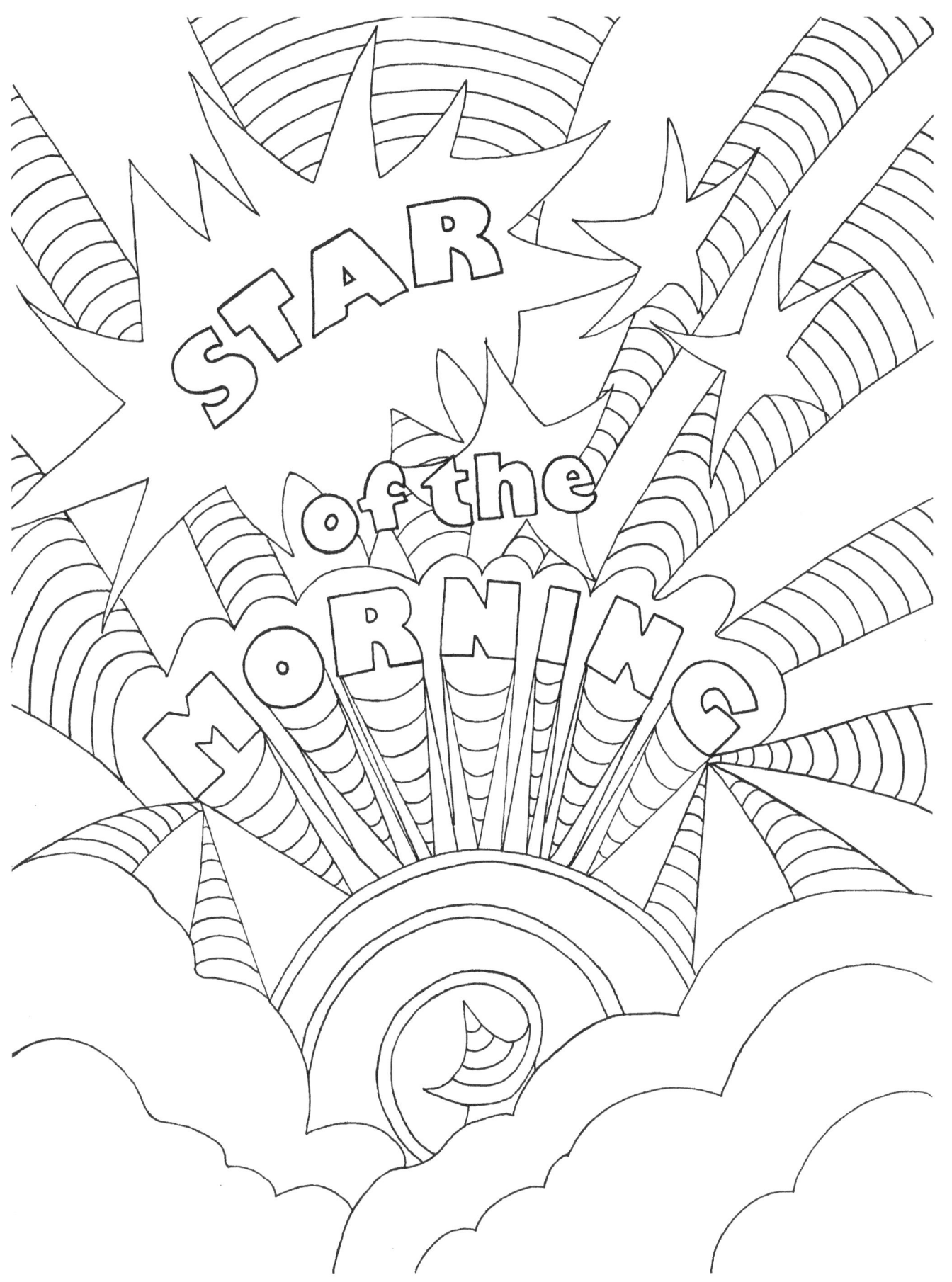

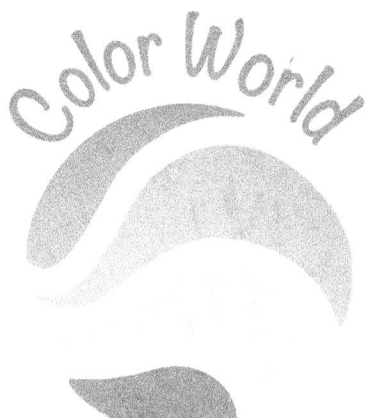

Count Your Blessings

1. ------------------------------

2. ------------------------------

3. ------------------------------

4. ------------------------------

5. ------------------------------

6. ------------------------------

7. ------------------------------

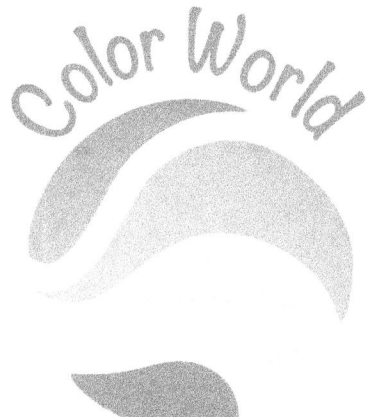

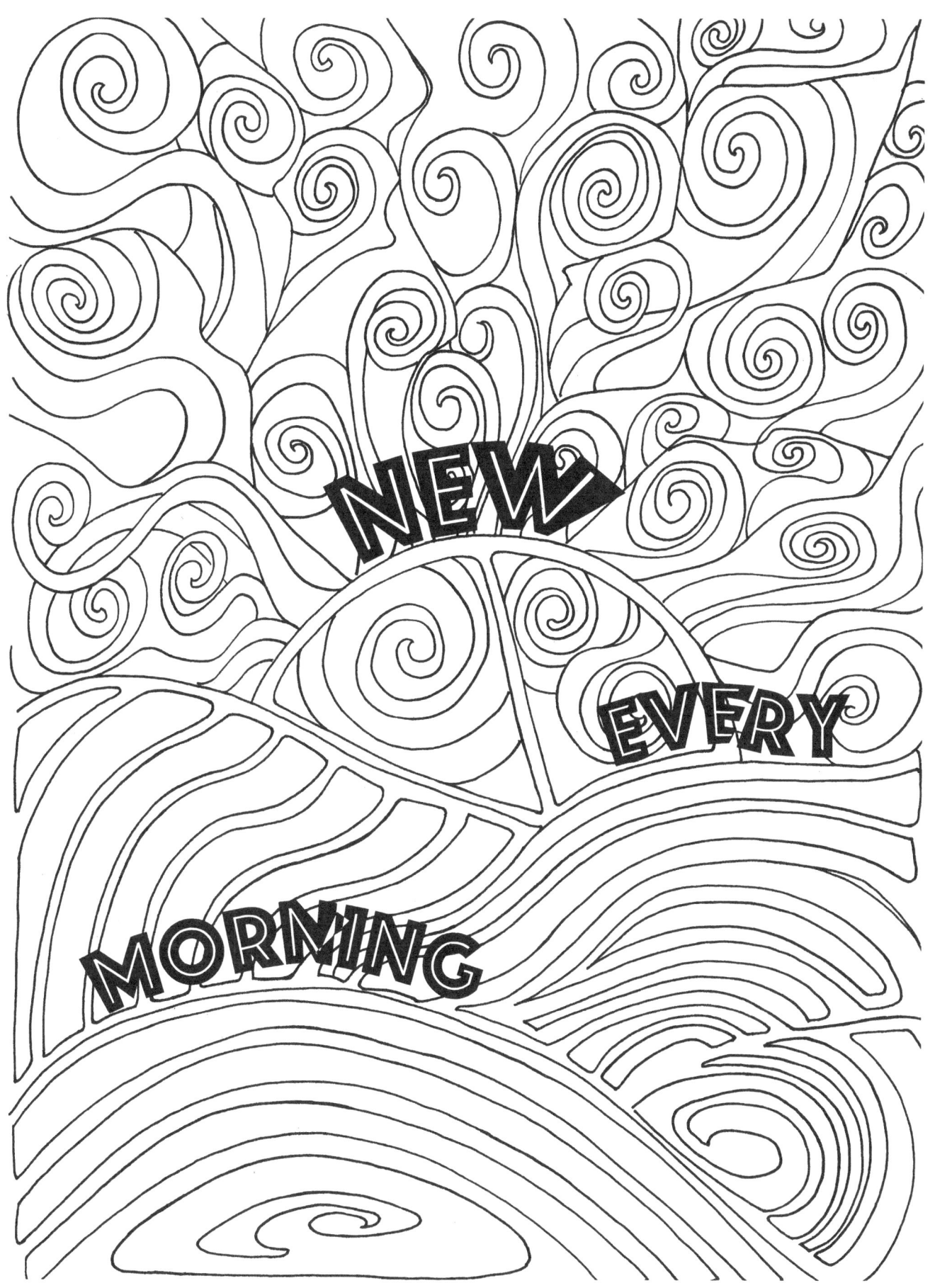

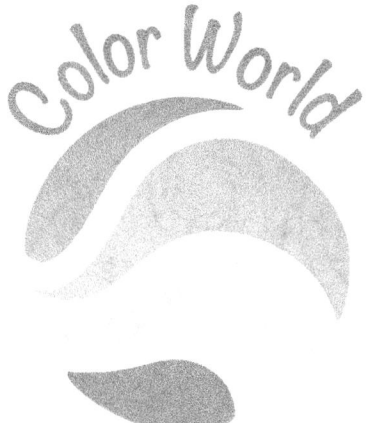

Cards for you to color and give to your loved ones!
Copy these cards onto heavy paper or cut them out and paste them onto blank cards.

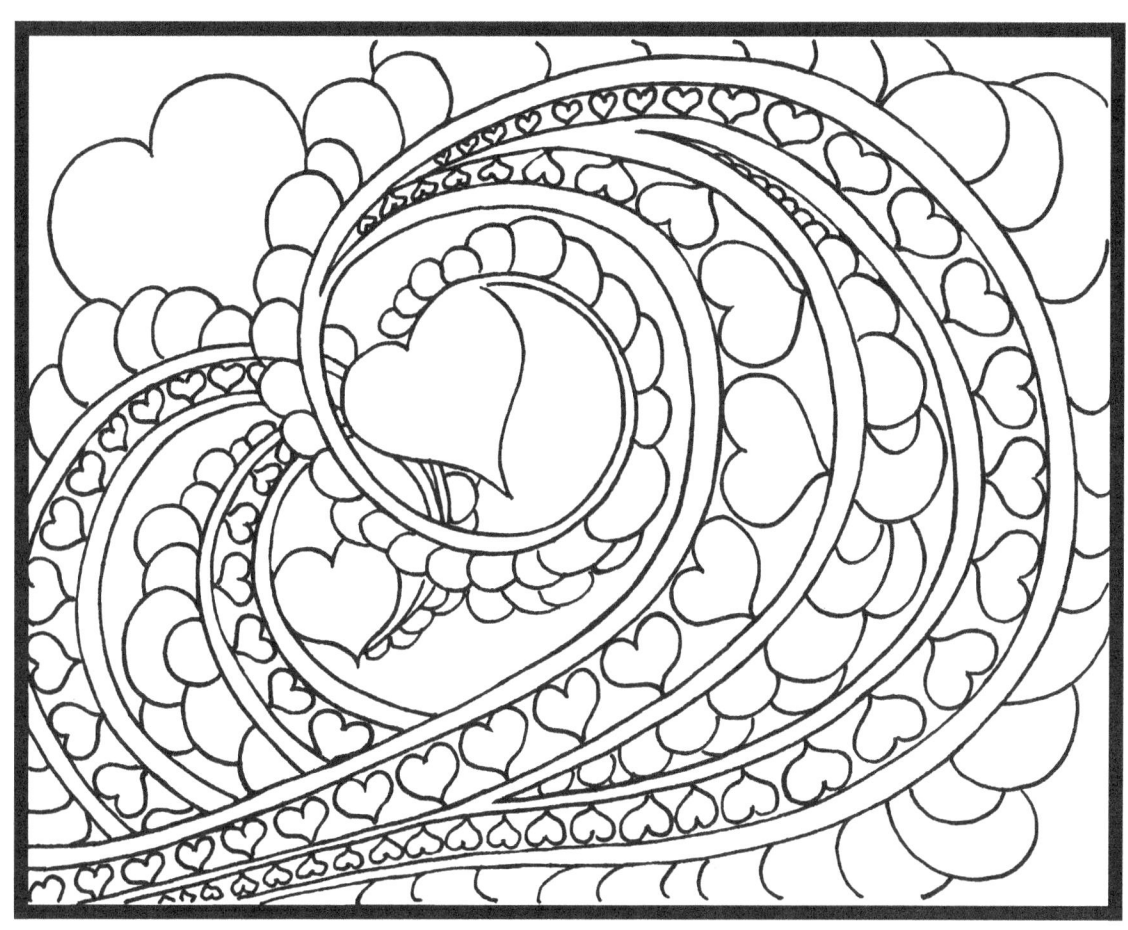

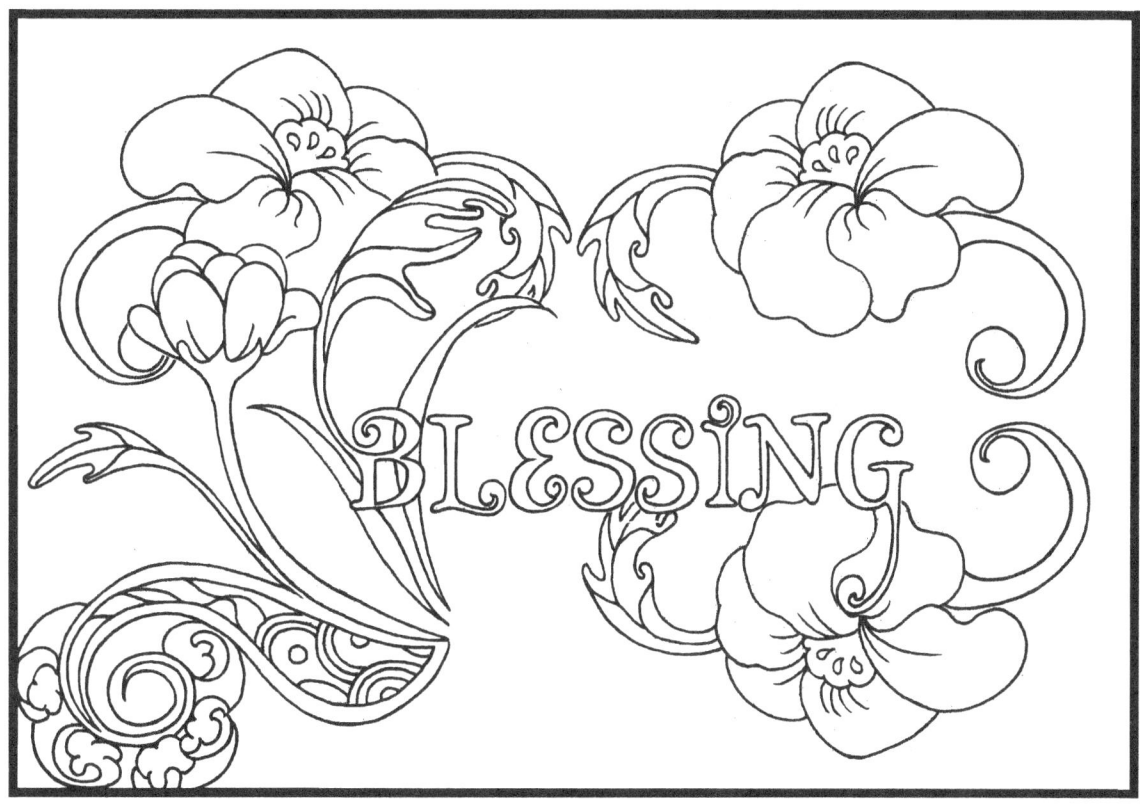

Color World

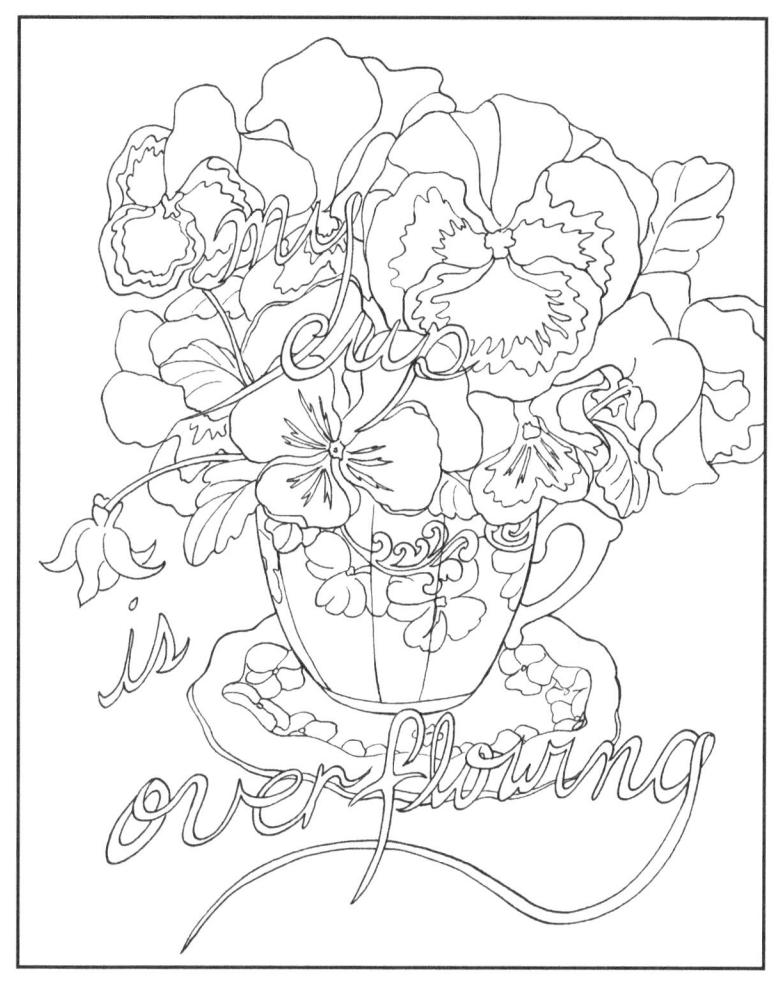

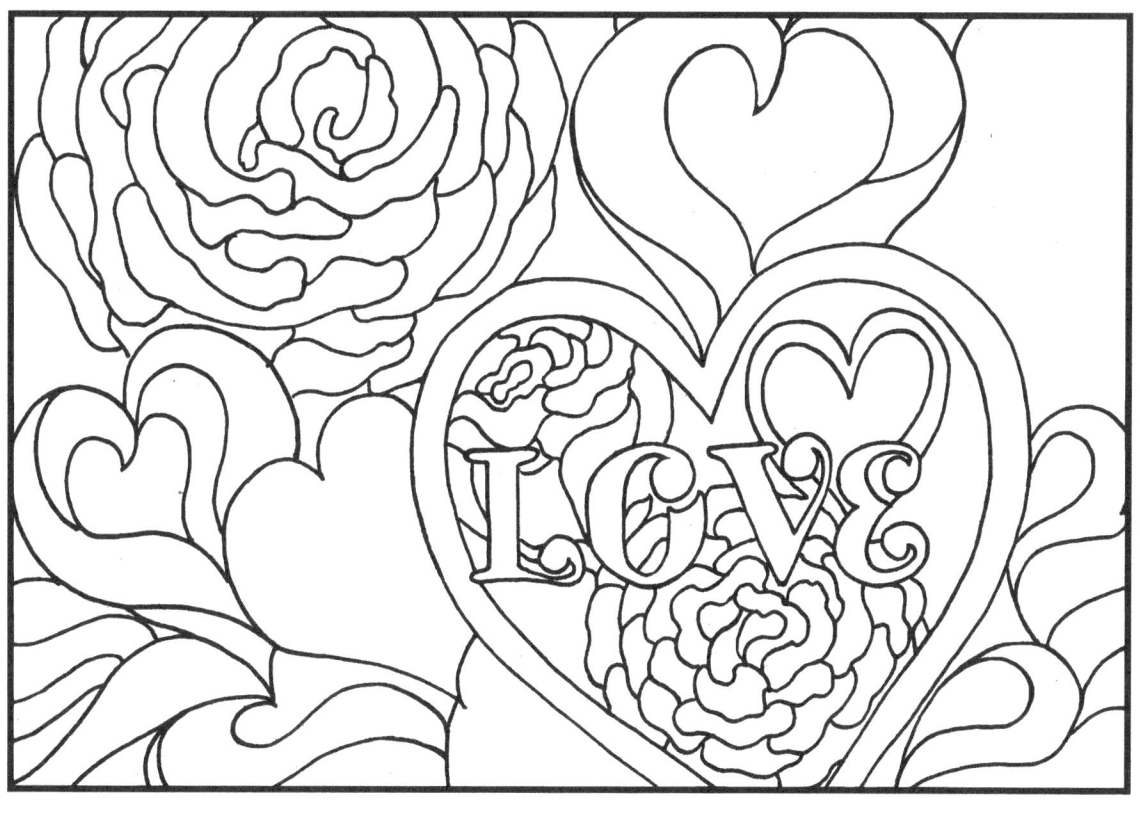

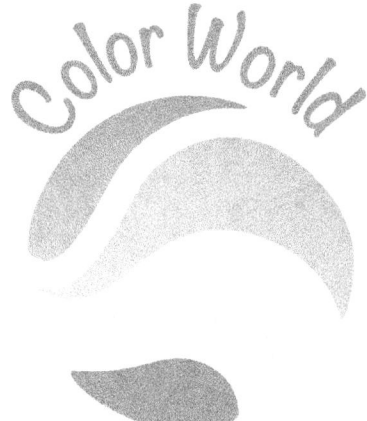

Thank you for choosing this book in the Color World series!

Would you like to download free, printable coloring pages? Would you like to know when more coloring books are available? Please visit rrrussellauthor.com/coloring-books to sign up for the Color World e-mail newsletter.

If you enjoy reading inspirational fiction about true love and big dreams against incredible odds, try *Venture Untamed* and the rest of the Venture series, written as R.H. Russell.

www.ingramcontent.com/pod-product-compliance
Lightning Source LLC
Chambersburg PA
CBHW081304180526

45170CB00007B/2565